CONVERSATIONS

CONVERSATIONS WITH

JEAN-PAUL SARTRE

PERRY ANDERSON

RONALD FRASER

QUINTIN HOARE

AND

SIMONE DE BEAUVOIR

Seagull
BOOKS

LONDON NEW YORK CALCUTTA

Seagull Books

Editorial offices:

1st Floor, Angel Court, 81 St Clements Court,
Oxford OX4 1AW, UK

1 Washington Square Village, Apt 1U, New York,
NY 10012, USA

26 Circus Avenue, Calcutta 700 017, India

Seagull Books 2006
Second Printing 2006

© New Left Review, London

ISBN 1 9054 2 201 6

British Library Cataloguing-in-Publication Data
A catalogue record for this book is available from the British Library

Typeset by Seagull Books, Calcutta, India
Printed in the United Kingdom by Biddles Ltd, King's Lynn

CONTENTS

ITINERARY OF A THOUGHT

How do you envisage the relationship between your early philosophical writings, above all L'Etre et Le Néant, *and your present theoretical work, from the* Critique de la Raison Dialectique *onwards? In the* Critique, *the typical concepts of* L'Etre et Le Néant *have disappeared, and a completely new vocabulary has taken their place. Yet when reading the passages of your forthcoming study of Flaubert published in* Les Temps Modernes *one is struck by the sudden re-emergence of the characteristic idiom of the early work—thetic consciousness, ego, nihilation, being, nothingness. These notions are now juxtaposed in the text with the distinct set of concepts which derive from the* Critique—*serialization, totalization, practico-inert, collectives. What is the precise relationship between the two in your current thought?*

The basic question here, of course, is my relationship to Marxism. I will try to explain autobiographically certain aspects of my early work, which may help to clarify the reasons why my outlook changed so fundamentally after the Second World War. A simple formula would be to say that life taught me *la force des choses*—the power of circumstances. In a way, *L'Etre et Le Néant* itself should have been the beginning of a discovery of this power of circumstances, since I had already been made a soldier, when I had not wanted to be one. Thus I had already encountered something that was not my freedom and which steered me from without. Then I was taken prisoner, a fate which I had sought to escape. Hence I started to learn what I have called human reality among things: Being-in-the-world.

Then, little by little, I found that the world was more complicated than this, for during the Resistance there appeared to be a possibility of free decision. For my state of mind during those years, I think that the first plays I wrote are very symptomatic: I called them a 'theatre of freedom'. The other day, I re-read a prefatory note of mine to a collection of these plays—*Les Mouches, Huis Clos* and others—and was truly scandalized. I had written: 'Whatever the circumstances, and wherever the site, a man is always free to choose to be a traitor or not . . .' When I read this, I said to myself: it's incredible, I actually believed that!

To understand how I could have done so, you must remember that there was a very simple problem during the Resistance—ultimately, only a question of courage. One had to accept the risks involved in what one was doing, that is, of being imprisoned or deported. But beyond this? A Frenchman was either for the Germans or against them, there was no other option. The real political problems, of being 'for, but' or 'against, but', were not posed by this experience. The result was that I concluded that in any circumstances, there is always a possible choice. Which is false. Indeed, it is so false that I later wanted precisely to refute myself by creating a character in *Le Diable et Le Bon Dieu*, Heinrich, who cannot choose. He wants to choose, of course, but he cannot choose either the Church, which has abandoned the poor, or the poor, who have abandoned the Church. He is thus a living contradiction, who will never choose. He is totally conditioned by his situation.

However, I understood all this only much later. What the drama of the war gave me, as it did everyone who participated in it, was the experience of heroism. Not my own, of course—all I did was a few errands. But the militant in the Resistance who was caught and tortured became a myth for us. Such militants existed, of course, but they represented a sort of personal myth as well. Would we be able to hold out against torture too? The problem then was solely that of physical endurance—it was not the ruses of history or the paths of alienation. A man is tortured: what will he do? He either speaks or refuses to speak. This is what I mean by the experience of heroism, which is a false experience.

After the war came the true experience, that of *society*. But I think it was necessary for me to pass via the myth of heroism first. That is to say, the pre-war personage who was more or less Stendhal's egotistical individualist had to be plunged into circumstances against his will, yet where he still had the power to say yes or no, in order to encounter inextricable entanglements of the post-war years as a man totally conditioned by his social existence and yet sufficiently capable of decision to reassume all this conditioning and to become responsible for it. For the idea which I have never ceased to develop is that in the end one is always responsible for what is made of one. Even if one can do nothing else besides assume this responsibility. For I believe that a man can always make something out of what is made of him. This is the limit I would today accord to freedom: the small movement which makes of a totally conditioned social being someone who does not render back completely what his conditioning has given him. Which makes of Genet a poet when he had been rigorously conditioned to be a thief.

Perhaps the book where I have best explained what I mean by freedom is, in fact, *Saint Genet*. For Genet was made a thief, he said 'I am a thief', and this tiny change was the start of a process whereby he became a poet and then eventually a being no longer even on the margin of society, someone who no longer knows where he is, who falls silent. It cannot be a happy freedom, in a case like this. Freedom is not a triumph. For Genet, it simply marked out certain routes which were not initially given.

L'Etre et Le Néant traced an interior experience, without any co-ordination with the exterior experience of a petty-bourgeois intellectual, which had become historically catastrophic at a certain moment. For I wrote *L'Etre et Le Néant* after the defeat of France, after all. But catastrophes have no lessons, unless they are the culmination of a praxis. Then one can say, my action has failed. But the disaster which overwhelmed the country had taught us nothing. Thus, in *L'Etre et Le Néant*, what you could call 'subjectivity' is not what it would be for me now, the small margin in an operation whereby an interiorization re-exteriorizes itself in an act. But 'subjectivity' and 'objectivity' seem to me entirely useless notions today, anyway. I might still use the term 'objectivity', I suppose, but only to emphasize that everything is objective. The individual interiorizes his social determinations: he interiorizes the relations of production, the family of his childhood, the historical past, the contemporary institutions, and he then re-exteriorizes these in acts and options which necessarily refer us back to them. None of this existed in *L'Etre et Le Néant*.

In L'Etre et Le Néant, *you radically rejected the concept of the unconscious, saying that it was a philosophical contradiction. The model of consciousness in your early work effectively excludes any idea of it whatever. Consciousness is always transparent to itself, even if the subject creates a false screen of 'bad faith'. Since then, you have among other things written a film-script on Freud—*

I broke with Huston precisely because Huston did not understand what the unconscious was. That was the whole problem. He wanted to suppress it, to replace it with the pre-conscious. He did not want the unconscious at any price—

The question one would like to ask is how you conceive the precise theoretical statute of the work of Freud today? Given your class position, it is not perhaps so surprising that you did not discover Marx before the war. But how did you miss Freud? Surely the opaque evidence of the unconscious, its resistances, should have been accessible to you even then?

They are not exactly comparable to the class struggle.

The two questions are linked, however. The thought of both Marx and Freud is a theory of conditioning in exteriority. When Marx says: 'It matters little what the bourgeoisie thinks it does, the important thing is what it does', one could replace the 'bourgeoisie' by 'a hysteric', and the formula would be one of Freud. Having said this, I must try to recount my relationship to Freud's work biographically. I will begin by saying that I undoubtedly had a deep repugnance for psychoanalysis in my youth, which needs to be explained as much as my innocence of the class struggle. The fact that I was a petty-bourgeois was responsible for the latter; one might say that the fact that I was French was responsible for the former. There would certainly be a lot of truth in this. You must never forget the weight of Cartesian rationalism in France. When you have just taken the *bachot* at the age of 17, with the 'I think, therefore I am' of Descartes as your set text, and you open *The Psychopathology of Everyday Life*, and you read the famous episode of Signorelli with its substitutions, combinations and displacements, implying that Freud

was simultaneously thinking of a patient who had committed suicide and of certain Turkish mores, and so
on—when you read all that, your breath is simply
taken away.

Such investigations were completely outside my preoc-
cupations at the time, which were at bottom to provide
a philosophical foundation for realism. Which in my
opinion is possible today, and which I have tried to do
all my life. In other words, how to give man both his
autonomy and his reality among real objects, avoiding
idealism without lapsing into a mechanistic materialism. I posed the problem in this way because I was
ignorant of dialectical materialism, although I should
add that this later allowed me to assign certain limits
to it—to validate the historical dialectic while rejecting
a dialectic of nature, in the sense of a natural process
which produces and resolves man into an ensemble of
physical laws.

To return to Freud, however, I have to say that I was
incapable of understanding him because I was a
Frenchman with a good Cartesian tradition behind me,
imbued with a certain rationalism, and I was therefore

deeply shocked by the idea of the unconscious.
However, I will not say *only* this because I must add
that I remain shocked by what was inevitable in
Freud—the biological and physiological language with
which he underpinned thoughts which were not trans-
latable into without mediation. Right up to the time of
Fliess, as you know, he wrote physiological studies
designed to provide an equivalent of the cathexes and
equilibria he had found in psychoanalysis. The result is
that the manner in which he describes the psychoanalytic object suffers from a kind of mechanistic cramp.
This is not always true, for there are moments when he
transcends this. But in general this language produces
a *mythology* of the unconscious which I cannot accept. I
am completely in agreement with the *facts* of diguise
and repression, as facts. But the *words* 'repression', or
'drive'—words which express one moment a sort of
finalism and the next moment a sort of mechanism,
these I reject. Let us take the example of 'condensation', for instance, which is an ambivalent term in
Freud. One can interpret it simply as a phenomenon
of association, in the same way as your English
philosophers and psychologists of the 18th and 19th

centuries. Two images are drawn together externally, they condense and form a third: this is classical psychological atomism. But one can also interpret the term on the contrary as expressive of a finality. Condensation occurs because two images combined answer a desire, a need. This sort of ambiguity occurs again and again in Freud. The result is a strange representation of the unconscious as a set of rigorous mechanistic determinations, in any event a casuality, and at the same time as a mysterious finality, such that there are 'ruses' of the unconscious, as there are 'ruses' of history; yet it is impossible to reunite the two in the work of many analysts—at least early analysts. I think that there is always a fundamental ambiguity in them; the unconscious is one moment *another consciousness*, and the next moment *other than consciousness*. What is other than consciousness then becomes simply a mechanism.

Thus I would reproach psychoanalytic theory with being a syncretic and not a dialectical thought. The word 'complex', indeed, indicates this very evidently: interpenetration without contradiction. I agree, of course, that there may exist an enormous number of 'larval' contradictions within individuals, which are often translated in certain situations by interpenetrations and not by confrontations. But this does not mean these contradictions do not exist. The results of syncretism, on the contrary, can be seen in the idea of the Oedipus complex, for instance: the fact is that analysts manage to find everything in it, equally well the fixation on the mother, love of the mother, or hatred of the mother, as Melanie Klein argues. In other words, anything can be derived from it, since it is not *structured*. The consequence is that an analyst can say one thing and then the contrary immediately afterwards, without in any way worrying about lack of logic, since after all 'opposites interpenetrate'. A phenomenon can mean this, while its contrary can also mean the same thing. Psychoanalytic theory is thus a 'soft' thought. It has no dialectical logic to it. Psychoanalysts will tell me that this is because there is no such logic in reality. But this is precisely what I am not sure of: I am convinced that complexes exist, but I am not so certain that they are not structured.

In particular, I believe that if complexes are true structures, 'analytic scepticism' would have to be abandoned. What I call the 'affective scepticism' of psychoanalysts is the belief of so many of them that the relationship which unites two people is only a 'reference'
to an original relationship which is an absolute: an
allusion to a primal scene, incomparable and unforget-
table—yet forgotten—between father and mother.
Ultimately, any sentiment experienced by an adult
becomes for the analyst a sort of occasion for the
rebirth of another. Now, there is a real truth in this:
the fixation of a girl on an older man may well come
from her father, or the fixation of a young man on a
girl may derive from a profusion of original relationships. But what is missing in conventional psychoanalytic accounts is the idea of dialectical irreducibility. In
a truly dialectical theory, such as historical materialism,
phenomena derive from each other dialectically: there
are different configurations of dialectical reality, and
each of these configurations is rigorously conditioned
by the previous one, while preserving and superseding
it at the same time. This supersession is, however, precisely irreducible. While one configuration may pre-

serve another, it can never simply be reduced to its predecessor. It is the idea of this *autonomy* that is lacking in psychoanalytic theory. A sentiment or a passion between two persons is certainly highly conditioned by their relationship to the 'primal object', and one can locate this object within it and explain the new relationship by it; but the relationship itself remains irreducible.

Thus there is an essential difference in my relationship to Marx and my relationship to Freud. When I discovered the class struggle, this was a *true* discovery, in which I now believe totally, in the very form of the descriptions which Marx gave to it. Only the epoch has changed; otherwise it is the same struggle with the same classes and the same road to victory. Whereas I do not believe in the unconscious in the form in which psychoanalysis presents it to us. In my present book on Flaubert, I have replaced my earlier notion of consciousness (although I still use the word a lot), with what I call *le vécu*—lived experience. I will try to describe in a moment what I mean by this term, which is neither the precautions of the preconscious, nor the unconscious, nor consciousness, but the terrain in which the individual is perpetually overflowed by himself and his riches and consciousness plays the trick of determining itself by forgetfulness.

In L'Etre et le Néant, there is not much room for the phenomenon of dreams. For Freud dreams were a privileged 'space' of the unconscious, the zone where psychoanalysis was discovered. Do you try to situate the space of dreams in your current works? This would be a concrete test of your present relationship to Freud.

My work on Flaubert deals with dreams. Unfortunately Flaubert himself reports very few of his dreams. But there are two extremely striking ones—both nightmares, which he recounts in *Mémoires d'un Fou,* an autobiography he wrote at the age of 17, and which are thus perhaps partly invented. One concerns his father, the other his mother: both reveal his relationship to his parents with an extraordinary evidence. The interesting thing, however, is that otherwise Flaubert virtually never mentions his parents in his writings. In fact, he had very bad relationships with both his father and mother, for a whole number of reasons which I try to analyse. He says nothing about them. They do not exist in his early works. The only time that he speaks of them, he speaks of them precisely where a psychoanalyst would like him to do, in the narrative of a dream. Yet it is Flaubert himself who spontaneously does so. Thereafter, at the very end of his life, five years before he died, he published a novella called *La Légende de Saint Julien l'Hospitalier*, which he said he had wanted to write for 30 years: it is in effect the story of a man who kills his father and his mother and who becomes a writer by doing so.

Thus Flaubert has two quite different conceptions of himself. One is at the level of banal description, for example when he writes to his mistress Louise: 'What am I? Am I intelligent or am I stupid? Am I sensitive or am I stolid? Am I mean or am I generous? Am I selfish or am I selfless? I have no idea, I suppose I am like everyone else, I waver between all these . . .' In other words, at this level he is completely lost. Why? Because none of these notions has any meaning in themselves. They only acquire a meaning from inter-subjectivity, in other words what I have called in the

Critique the 'objective spirit' within which each member of a group or society refers to himself and appears to others, establishing relations of interiority between persons which derive from the same information or the same context.

Yet one cannot say that Flaubert did not have, at the very height of his activity, a comprehension of the most obscure origins of his own history. He once wrote a remarkable sentence: 'You are doubtless like myself, you all have the same terrifying and tedious depths'— *les mêmes profoundeurs terribles et ennuyeuses*. What could be a better formula for the whole world of psycho-analysis, in which one makes terrifying discoveries, yet which always tediously come to the same thing? His awareness of these depths was not an intellectual one. He later wrote that he often had fulgurating intuitions, akin to a dazzling bolt of lightning in which one simul-taneously sees nothing and sees everything. Each time they went out, he tried to retrace the paths revealed to him by this blinding light, stumbling and falling in the subsequent darkness.

For me, these formulations define the relationship

which Flaubert had with what is ordinarily called the unconscious, and what I would call a total absence of knowledge, but a real comprehension. I distinguish here between comprehension and intellection: there can be intellection of a practical conduct, but only comprehension of a passion. What I call *le vécu*—lived experience—is precisely the ensemble of the dialectical process of psychic life, in so far as this process is obscure to itself because it is a constant totalization, thus necessarily a totalization which cannot be conscious of what it is. One can be conscious of an external totalization, but one cannot be conscious of a totalization which also totalizes consciousness. 'Lived experience', in this sense, is perpetually susceptible of comprehension, but never of knowledge. Taking it as a point of departure, one can know certain psychic phenomena by concepts, but not this experience itself. The highest form of comprehension of lived experience can forge its own language—which will always be inadequate, and yet which will often have the metaphorical structure of the dream itself. Comprehension of a dream occurs when a man can express it in a language which is itself dreamt. Lacan says that the unconscious is structured like a language. I would say that the language which expresses it has the structure of a dream. In other words, comprehension of the unconscious in most cases never achieves explicit expression. Flaubert constantly speaks of *l'indisable,* which means the 'unsayable', only the word does not exist in French, it should be *l'indicible* (perhaps it was a regional usage in Flaubert's time, but in any case it is not the normal word). The 'unsayable', however, was something very definite for him. When he gave his autobiography to his mistress at the age of 25, he wrote to her: 'You will suspect all the unsayable.' Which did not mean family secrets or anything like that. Of course, he hated his elder brother, but this is not what he was talking about. He meant precisely this kind of comprehension of oneself which cannot be named and which perpetually escapes one.

The conception of 'lived experience' marks my change since *L'Etre et Le Néant*. My early work was a rationalist philosophy of consciousness. It was all very well for me to dabble in apparently non-rational processes in the individual, the fact remains that *L'Etre et le Néant* is a monument of rationality. But in the end it becomes an irrationalism, because it cannot account rationally for those processes which are 'below' consciousness and which are also rational, but lived as irrational. Today, the notion of 'lived experience' represents an effort to preserve that presence to itself which seems to me indispensable for the existence of any psychic fact, while at the same time this presence is so opaque and blind before itself that it is also an absence from itself. Lived experience is always simultaneously present to itself and absent from itself. In developing this notion, I have tried to surpass the traditional psychoanalytic ambiguity of psychic facts which are both teleological and mechanical, by showing that every psychic fact involves an intentionality which aims at something, while among them a certain number can only exist if they are comprehended, but neither named nor known. The latter include what I call the 'stress' of a neurosis. A neurosis is in the first instance a specific wound, a defective structure which is a certain way of living a childhood. But this is only the initial wound: it is then patched up and bandaged by a system which covers and soothes the wound, and which then like

anti-bodies in certain cases, suddenly does something
abominable to the organism. The unity of this system
is the neurosis. The work of its 'stress' is intentional,
but it cannot be seized as such without disappearing. It
is precisely for this reason that if it is transferred into
the domain of knowledge, by analytic treatment, it can
no longer be reproduced in the same manner.

*There is an obvious question raised by your work on Flaubert.
You have already written a study of Baudelaire—*

—A very inadequate, an extremely bad one—

*Then a long book on Genet, after that an essay on Tintoretto
and then an autobiography,* Les Mots. *After this succession
of writings, what will be the methodological novelty of the
book on Flaubert? Why exactly did you decide to return once
again to the project of explaining a life?*

In the *Question de Méthode*, I discussed the different
mediations and procedures which could permit an
advance in our knowledge of men if they were taken
together. In fact, everyone knows and everyone admits,
for instance, that psychoanalysis and Marxism should
be able to find the mediations necessary to allow a

combination of the two. Everyone adds, of course, that psychoanalysis is not primary, but that correctly coupled and rationalized with Marxism, it can be useful. Likewise, everyone says that there are American sociological notions which have a certain validity, and that sociology in general should be used—not, of course, the Russian variety which is no more than an enumeration or nomenclature. Everyone agrees on all this. Everyone in fact *says* it—but who has tried to *do* it?

I myself was in general only repeating these irreproachable maxims in *Question de Méthode*. The idea of the book on Flaubert was to abandon these theoretical disquisitions, because they were ultimately getting us nowhere, and to try to give a concrete example of how it might be done. The result can look after itself. Even if it is a failure, it can thereby give others the idea of redoing it, better. For the question the book seeks to answer is: How shall I study a man with all these methods, and how in this study will these methods condition each other and find their respective place?

You feel you did not have these keys when you wrote Saint Genet, *for example?*

No, I did not have them all. It is obvious that the study
of the conditioning of Genet at the level of institutions
and of history is inadequate—very, very inadequate.
The main lines of the interpretation, that Genet was
an orphan of Public Assistance, who was sent to a peasant home and who owned nothing, remain true,
doubtless. But all the same, this happened in 1925 or
so and there was a whole context to this life which is
quite absent. The Public Assistance, a foundling represents a specific social phenomenon, and anyway Genet
is a product of the 20th century; yet none of this is
registered in the book.

Whereas today I would like the reader to feel the presence of Flaubert the whole time; my ideal would be
that the reader simultaneously feels, comprehends and
knows the personality of Flaubert, totally as an individual and yet totally as an expression of his time. In
other words, Flaubert can only be understood by his
difference from his neighbours.

Do you see what I mean by this? For example, there
were a considerable number of writers who elaborated
analogous theories at the time and produced more or

less valid works inspired by them, Leconte de Lisle or the Goncourts, for example: it is necessary to try to study how they were all determined to produce this particular vision, and how Flaubert was determined similarly yet otherwise, and saw it in another fashion. My aim is to try to demonstrate the encounter between the development of the person, as psychoanalysis has shown it to us, and the development of history. For at a certain moment, an individual in his very deepest and most intimate conditioning, by the family, can fulfill a historical role. Robespierre could be taken as an example, for instance. But it would be impossible to pursue such a study of him, because there are no materials for doing so. What would be necessary to know is what was the encounter of the revolution which created the Committee of Public Safety, and the son of Monsieur and Madame Robespierre of Arras.

This is the theoretical aim of your present work. But why exactly the choice of Flaubert?

Because he is the imaginary. With him, I am at the border, the barrier of dreams.

There have been writers or politicians who have left a certain work and who could equally well provide the material for such a study—

In theory, yes. There were a number of reasons, however, which led me to select Flaubert. Firstly, to give the strictly circumstantial cause of this selection: Flaubert is one of the very rare historical or literary personages who have left behind so much information about themselves. There are no less that 13 volumes of correspondence, each of 600 pages or so. He often wrote letters to several persons the same day, with slight variations between them, which are often very amusing. Apart from this, there are numerous reports and witnesses of him; the Goncourt brothers kept a diary and saw Flaubert very frequently, so that we see him from the outside through the Goncourts and we also have a record of what he said to others about himself, recorded by the Goncourts—not an altogether trustworthy source, of course, since they were rancorous imbeciles in many ways. Nevertheless, there are many facts in their Journal. Besides this, of course, there is a complete correspondence with George Sand, letters of George Sand on Flaubert, memoirs of him, and so on.

All this is completely circumstantial, but it is of great importance.

Secondly, however, Flaubert represents for me the exact opposite of my own conception of literature: a total disengagement and a certain idea of form, which is not that which I admire. For example, Stendhal is a writer whom I greatly prefer to Flaubert, while Flaubert is probably much more important for the development of the novel than Stendhal. I mean that Stendhal is much finer and stronger. One can give oneself completely to him—his style is acceptable, his heroes are sympathetic, his vision of the world is true and the historical conception behind it is very acute. There is nothing like this in Flaubert. Only, Flaubert is much more significant than Stendhal for the history of the novel. If Stendhal had not existed, it would still have been possible to go straight from Laclos to Balzac. Whereas, let us say, Zola or the Nouveau Roman are inconceivable without Flaubert. Stendhal is greatly loved by the French, but his influence on the novel is minimal. Flaubert's influence by contrast is immense, and for this reason alone it is important to study him.

Given that, he began to fascinate me precisely because I saw him in every way as the contrary of myself. I found myself wondering: 'How was he possible?' For I then rediscovered another dimension of Flaubert, which is besides the very source of his talent. I was used to reading Stendhal and company, where one is in complete accord with the hero, whether he is Julien Sorel or Fabrice.

Reading Flaubert one is plunged into persons with whom one is in complete disaccord, who are irksome. Sometimes one feels with them, and then somehow they suddenly reject one's sympathy and one finds oneself once again antagonistic to them. Obviously it was this that fascinated me, because it made me curious. This is precisely Flaubert's art. It is clear that he detested himself, and when he speaks of his principal characters, he has a terrible attitude of sadism and masochism towards them: he tortures them because they are himself, and also to show that other people and the world torture him. He also tortures them because they are not him and he is anyway vicious and sadistic and wants to torture others. His unfortunate characters have very little luck, submitted to all this.

At the same time, Flaubert writes from within his characters and is always speaking of himself in a certain fashion. He thus succeeds in speaking of himself in a way that is unique. This type of discomfited, refused confession, with its self-hatred, its constant reversion to things he comprehends without knowing, wanting to be completely lucid and yet always grating—Flaubert's testimony about himself is something exceptional, which had never been seen before and has not been seen since. This is another motive for studying him.

The third reason for choosing Flaubert is that he represents a sequel to *L'Imaginaire*. You may remember that in my very early book *L'Imaginaire* I tried to show that an image is not a sensation reawakened, or reworked by the intellect, or even a former perception altered and attenuated by knowledge, but is something entirely different—an absent reality, focused in its absence through what I called an *analogon*: that is to say, an object which serves as an analogy and is traversed by an intention. For example, when you are going to sleep, the little dots in your eyes—phosphenes—may serve as an analogy for every kind of oneiric or hypnagogic image. Between waking and sleeping, some people see vague shapes pass, which are phosphenes through which they focus on an imagined person or a thing. In *L'Imaginaire*, I tried to prove that imaginary objects—images—are an absence. In my book on Flaubert, I am studying imaginary persons—people who like Flaubert act out roles. A man is like a leak of gas, escaping into the imaginary. Flaubert did so perpetually; yet he also had to see reality because he hated it, so there is the whole question of the relationship between the real and the imaginary which I try to study in his life and work.

Finally, via all this, it is possible to ask the question: what was the *imaginary social world* of the dreamy bourgeoisie of 1848? This is an intriguing subject in itself. Between 1830 and 1840 Flaubert was in a Lycée in Rouen, and all his texts speak of his fellow-pupils there are contemptible, mediocre bourgeois. It so happens, however, that there were five years of violent, historic fights in the lycées of that time! After the revolution of 1830, there were boys who launched political struggles in the schools, who fought and were defeated. The reading of the romantics of which Flaubert speaks so often as a challenge to their parents, is only explicable in this perspective: when these youths finally become *blasés*, they have been reciperated as 'ironic' bourgeois, and they have failed. The extraordinary thing is that Flaubert does not say a word about any of this. He simply describes the boys who surround him as if they were future adults—in other words, abject. He writes: 'I saw defects which would become vices, needs which would become manias, follies which would become crimes—in short, children would become men.' The only history of the school for him was the passage from childhood to maturity. The reality is, however, that this history was that of a bourgeoisie seized with shame at itself in its sons, of the defeat of these sons and thereby the suppression of its shame. The end result of this history will be the massacre of 1848.

Before 1830, the bourgeoisie was hiding under its blankets. When it finally emerged, its sons cried 'Bravo! We are going to declare the Republic,' but their fathers found they needed an eiderdown after all. Louis-Phillipe became king. The sons persuaded them-

selves their fathers had been duped, and continued
the struggle. The result was an uproar in the schools:
in vain, they were expelled. In 1831, when Louis-
Phillipe dismisses Lafayette and the road to reaction is
open, there were boys of 13 or 14 in Flaubert's school,
who calmly refused to go to confession, having decided
that this was an excellent pretext for a confrontation
with the authorities, since after all the bourgeoisie was
still officially Voltairean. Confession was a survival from
Louis XVIII and Charles X, and raised awkward questions about compulsory religious instruction, which
might eventually get as far as the Chamber of
Deputies. I take off my hat to these boys of 14 who
planned this strategy, knowing very well that they
would be expelled from the school. The chaplain
descended on them—'Confess!' 'No!'—then another
functionary—'No, No, No!'—they were taken to the
principal and thrown out of the school. Whereupon
there was a gigantic uproar in the whole college, which
was what they had hoped for. The fourth year class
threw rotten eggs at the vice-principal, and two more
boys were expelled. Then the day-boys of the class met
at dawn and took an oath to avenge their comrades.

The next day at six in the morning, the boarders opened the doors to them. Together, they seized and occupied the building. Already, in 1831! From their fortress there, they bombarded the Academic Council which was deliberating in another building within reach of their windows.

The principal was meanwhile throwing himself at the feet of the older pupils, imploring them not to solidarize with the occupation—successfully. Eventually, the fourth year class did not achieve the reinstatement of their comrades, but the authorities had to promise that there would be no sanctions against them for the occupation. Three days later, they found they had been tricked: the college was closed for two months. Exactly like today.

The next year, when they came back, they were naturally raging and there was constant turbulence in the Lycée. This was the time in which Flaubert lived, and yet he did not experience it like that. He wrote a great deal about his childhood and youth—but there is not a single text which refers to this history. In fact, what happened, of course, was that he lived the same evolution of this generation in his own way. He was unaffected by this violent episode and yet he arrived at the same result by a different route somewhat later. The philosophy teacher in the school fell ill, and a substitute took over for him. The pupils decided the substitute was an incompetent and made life impossible for him. The principal tried to victimize two or three, and the whole class solidarized with them: Flaubert now wrote their collective letter to the principal, denouncing the quality of the course and the threats of punishment. The upshot was that he and two or three others were expelled from the school. The meaning of the protest this time is very clear: Flaubert and his class-mates were young bourgeois demanding a proper bourgeois education—'Our fathers are paying enough, after all'. The evolution of a generation and of a class are manifest in this second episode. These different experiences produce a bitter literature on the bourgeoisie and then this generation resigns itself to becoming merely ironic—another way of being bourgeois.

Why have you opted for biography and the theatre in recent years, and abandoned the novel? Is it that you think

Marxism and psychoanalysis have rendered the novel as a form impossible, by the weight of their concepts?

I have often asked myself that question. It is, in fact, true that there is no technique that can account for a character in a novel as one can account for a real person, who has existed, by means of a Marxist or psychoanalytic interpretation. But if an author has recourse to these two systems within a novel, without an adequate formal device for doing so, the novel disappears. These devices are lacking, and I do not know if they are possible.

You think that the existence of Marxism and of psychoanalysis prevents any novelist from writing, so to speak, naively today?

By no means. But if he does so, the novel will all the same be classified as 'naïve'. In other words, a natural universe of the novel will not exist, only a certain specific type of novel—the 'spontaneous', 'naïve' novel. There are excellent examples of the latter, but the author who writes them has to make a conscious decision to ignore these interpretative techniques. Thereby he necessarily becomes less naïve. There is another type of novel today in which the work is conceived as a sort of infernal machine—fake novels like those of Gombrowicz, for example. Gombrowicz is aware of psychoanalysis, and of Marxism and many other things, but he remains sceptical about them, and hence constructs objects which destroy themselves in their very act of construction—creating a model for what might be a novel with an analytic and materialist foundation.

Why have you personally stopped writing novels?

Because I have felt no urge to do so. Writers have always more or less chosen the imaginary. They have a need for a certain ration of fiction. Writing on Flaubert is enough for me by way of fiction—it might indeed be called a novel. Only I would like people to say that it was a true novel. I try to achieve a certain level of comprehension of Flaubert by means of hypotheses. Thus I use fiction—guided and controlled, but nonetheless fiction—to explore why, let us say, Flaubert wrote one thing on the 15th March and the exact opposite on the 21st March, to the same correspondent, without worrying about the contradiction. My hypotheses are in this sense a sort of invention of the personage.

You have reproached a book like The Children of Sanchez *for not being a literary work because the people in it speak a language like that of all of us when we are not writers. You think such works lack invention?*

The Children of Sanchez is not a literary work, but it renders a mass of literary works redundant. Why write a novel on its characters or their milieu? They tell us much more by themselves, with a much greater self-understanding and eloquence. The book is not literature because there is no quest for a form that is also a meaning in it: for me the two—form and meaning—are always linked. There is no production of an object, a constructed object.

You continue to write plays?

Yes, because plays are something else again. For me the theatre is essentially a myth. Take the example of a petty-bourgeois and his wife who quarrel with each other the whole time. If you tape their disputes, you will record not only the two of them, but the petty-bourgeoisie and its world, what society has made of it, and so on. Two or three such studies and any possible novel on the life of a petty-bourgeois couple would be outclassed. By contrast, the relationship between man and woman as we see it in Strindberg's *Dance of Death* will never be outclassed. The subject is the same, but taken to the level of myth. The playwright presents to men the *eidos* of their daily existence: their own life in such a way that they see it as if externally. This was the genius of Brecht, indeed. Brecht would have protested violently if anyone said to him that his plays were myths. Yet what else is *Mother Courage*—an anti-myth that despite itself becomes a myth?

You discussed the theatre with Brecht?

I saw Brecht three or four times in a political context, but we never had a chance to discuss the theatre. I admire Brecht's plays very much, but I think that what Brecht said about them is not always true. His theory of *Entfremdung*—distanciation—is one thing: the actual relationship between the public and his characters is another. The blind and deaf girl in *Mother Courage* calls to the people when she falls from the roof, dying. This is a scene of pathos, and yet it is precisely a passage of the play where Brecht most wants to establish a contestation and recoil from the drama. Mother

Courage herself is an anti-heroine who—unavoidably, by her very mystification—becomes a heroine. The *Caucasian Chalk Circle* presents the same paradox— scenes such as the flight of the servant or the adjudication of the child, which despite all Brecht's efforts are extremely moving in the most classical tradition of the theatre. Brecht was tremendously astute in his use of theatre, but he could not always control the final result of his writing.

The Critique de la Raison Dialectique *appears to be constructed on the idea that there is a fundamental homogeneity between the individual and history: the central theme of the book is the reversible relationships—interversions—between the individual, worked matter, the group, the series, the practico-inert, collectives. To adopt its vocabulary, your formal aim is to show how the totalizing acts of every individual are totalized in exteriority by others and become other to their agents, just as groups become other to themselves through serialization. The* Critique *deals in a very systematic way with that aspect of history which presents itself as alienation and degradation of intentional projects, whether by individuals or groups, in their encounter with materiality and alterity, in the world of scarcity. There is, however, another aspect of history which is not accounted for by the* Critique. *Social facts are not simply a totalization in exteriority of the totalizing acts of a multiplicity of individuals and groups, which may during certain privileged moments achieve an apocalyptic sovereignty, but which normally fall into the practico-inert. They have an intrinsic order of their own, which is not deducible from the criss-crossing of innumerable individual totalizations. The most obvious example of this is language— which can in no way be described as a simple totalization of all the speech-acts of linguistic agents. The subject who speaks never totalizes linguistic laws by his words. Language has its own intelligibility as a system which appears heterogeneous to the subject. Can the themes of 'totalization' and the 'practico-inert' ever account for the emergence of ordered social structures, not merely random alienation of subjective projects?*

But there is totalization in language. You cannot say a single sentence which does not refer, by its elements, to opposites. Thereby the whole of language, as a system of differential meanings, is present in its very absence, as linguists themselves admit. Every sentence is a levy on the entire resources of speech, for words

41

only exist by their opposition to each other. There is thus certainly totalization in language.

The question is whether there is only totalization? There are two central examples in the Critique *of a multiplicity of totalizations which fall into the practico-inert and become an alien power denaturing the intentions of their agents. One is that of different Chinese peasants cutting down trees to enlarge their cultivation of land, thus creating erosion, which thereby causes floods which then ruin their lands. The other is of the impact of gold in 16th-century Spain—whereby the individual decisions of each single producer to raise prices caused an uncontrollable general inflation which eventually resulted in the collective impoverishment of all of them. These two examples do not have the same type of intelligibility—*

I agree. The deforestation of the Chinese peasants is a product of individuals, each acting on their own, directly on nature, in ignorance of the others. They are not united by any collective object, and it is only gradually that the end-result of their acts imposes itself on them. The counter-finality of these peasants is cultural, but it concerns above all the relationship of a multiplicity of individuals with nature. Whereas the impact of gold in Spain presupposes money, which is a social institution. Money has nothing natural about it, it is a conventional system in some ways very similar to language. Thus gold is a pre-eminently social fact. I therefore am perfectly in agreement that there is a specific reality of social facts. This reality implies precisely that every totalization of the individual in relation to this reality either fails, is deviated by it or is a negative totalization. When I speak, I never say completely what I want to say and I often do not know what I say, given that my words are robbed from me and revealed to me as other than what I intended. But the important thing is that these social facts are, in spite of everything, the product of the social activity of collective ensembles. I will be discussing this in the second volume of the *Critique*. Language exists only as a convention.

But where does the order of this convention come from? To ask the same question in a different way: by the end of the Critique *the reader has been taken through all the different reversible relationships of individuals, groups, series and the practico-inert, which constitute for you 'the formal elements of any history'. Yet from this perspective there seems to be no reason why history should not then be an arbitrary chaos of inter-blocking projects, a sort of colossal traffic-jam?*

There are a number of reasons. The first is that accumulation exists. There are crucial domains where accumulation occurs: science, capital, goods—which thereby produce a history: change. This is something different from a mere transition. There are periods which are transitions, until something is invented that changes. For example, the whole feudal period of the 11th, 12th and 13th centuries is a perpetual turmoil: there were events everywhere, yet there was no emergence from the Middle Ages because the elements for doing so did not exist. Then, one day, a certain number of processes coincided, social and economic facts like the indebtedness of the lords, the run of the Church, the change in the nature of Catholicism, the peasant revolts, scientific discoveries, and a spiral development of history resulted. Science, of course, in a sense advanced in a straight line through all its conversions, hesitations and errors. These mistakes and confusions might be classified as 'subjective'—they have little importance in the development of science. On the other hand, they whirl about every level of science and deform its discoveries and practices, changing them into other than themselves: a discovery made because of war in time of war will serve in peace, while a discovery in time of peace will serve for war. Simultaneously, there are whole plateaux where the class struggle changes because there is a new mode of production. I have not discussed any of this in the first volume of the *Critique*, both because I believe in the general schema provided by Marx and because I intend to study it at the level of history proper. For it is at the level of history that one should determine to what extent there is or is not progress, to what extent progress exists only where there is accumulation, and whether it produces in its train total modifications which are not necessarily progressive.

What is going to be the architecture of the second volume of the Critique?

I will simply try to show the dialectical intelligibility of a movement of historical temporalization.

A movement?

The movement. The difference between the first and second volume is this: the first is an abstract work where I show the possibilities of exchange, degradation, the practico-inert, series, collectives, recurrence and so on. It is concerned only with the theoretical possibilities of their combinations. The object of the second volume is history itself. But I know no other history than our own, so the question 'What is history?' becomes 'What is our history?'—the history in which Mahomet was born and not one in which he never lived. It is irrelevant to wonder whether there are other histories in other galaxies. Perhaps there are, but we know nothing of them, and they consequently have no importance to us. Thus all the notions which will emerge from the second volume will be rigorously applied to our own history; my aim will be to prove that there is a dialectical intelligibility of the singular. For ours is a singular history. It is determined by the forces of production and the relations of production, their correspondences and their conflicts. It is possible that in completely primitive societies there exist the 'global facts' of which Mauss speaks—a kind of undifferentiated social conditioning. But even if this were so, it is not the history that I will be studying. What I will seek to show is the dialectical intelligibility of that which is not universalisable.

It is still very difficult to see how a multiplicity of individual acts can ever give birth to social structures which have their own laws, discontinuous *from the acts which for you formally constitute a historical dialectic? A tribe can speak a language for centuries and then be discovered by an anthropologist who can decipher its phonological laws, which have been forever unknown to the totality of the subjects speaking the language. How can these objective laws be deduced merely from words spoken?*

I believe that all the same language is a totalized and detotalized result of the ensemble of human activities during a certain time. Language is imposed on each of us as a practico-inert.

The connotation of 'practico-inert' is precisely that of a brute, random mass alien to human agents. The problem is, how does this mass happen to have a rigorous structure—the laws of grammar or, more fundamentally, the relations of production? These structures are never intentional objects—they are heterogeneous to the historical acts of individuals?

There is a historical problem of the passage from non-language to language in early human communities: it is impossible to reconstruct this passage, but probably it was accomplished within certain early institutions. For language sustains institutions, institutions are a language, and language is itself an institution. From the moment that a limited system of signs exists, which has an institutional character, both invented by the group and already dividing the group, language can change men into collectives. I have tried to explain this in the *Critique*. An institution or collective object is always a product of the activity of the group in *matter*, whether verbal matter or physico-chemical matter, and is thereby sealed and surpassed by an inertia which separates the group and imposes itself on it as the instituted and sacred. The subjective here capsizes into the objective and the objective into the subjective: the result is an instituted object. Thus I am in complete agreement that social facts have their own structures and laws that dominate individuals, but I only see in this the reply of worked matter to the agents who work it.

Why is this 'reply' a coherent discourse?

For me the fact of being worked does not endow matter with a system, but the fact of becoming inert converts work into a system.

Not everything that is inert is a system.

Structures are created by activity which has no structure, but suffers its results as a structure.

How can individual acts result in ordered structures, and not a tangled labyrinth—unless you believe in a sort of pre-established harmony between them?

You are forgetting the level of power and therefore of generality. If a decision is taken at a certain level of political or religious power, an objective unity is given by the project at that level. What then happens is that others deviate and deform the project, but they simultaneously create something else by their work: other structures with their own internal relations which constitute a queer kind of object, but a potent and significant one. In the last chapter of the *Critique*, entitled 'Towards History', I started to discuss this problem. I tried to argue that an object created by a plurality of different or antagonistic groups is nevertheless, in the very moment of their shock against each other, intelligible. In the second volume, I was going to take the elementary example of a battle, which remains intelligible after the confusion of the two armies engaged in combat in it. From there I planned to develop a study of the objects constituted by entire collectivities with their own interests. In particular I want to analyse the example of Stalin to see how the objects which constituted Stalinist institutions were created through the ensemble of relationships between groups and within groups in Soviet society, and through the relationship of all these to Stalin and of Stalin to them. Finally, I was going to end by studying the unity of objects in a society completely rent asunder by class struggle, and considering several classes and their actions to show how these objects were completely deviated and always represented a detotalization while at the same time preserving a determinate intelligibility. Once one has reached this, one has reached history. Hence I had the embryo of an answer to the question you have been asking me. There is an institutional order which is necessarily—unless we are to believe in God the father or an organicist mythology—the product of masses of men constituting a social unity and which at the same time is radically distinct from all of them, becoming an implacable demand and an ambiguous means of communication and non-communication between them. Aesop once said that language is both. The same is true of institutions. Indeed, I would like to write a study of work and technology to show exactly what happens to material in industry, how it becomes an inhuman image of man, by its demands. For I believe that the existence of different ethics in different epochs is due to matter: it is because of inert, inanimate objects that there are demands in us. A demand is fixed and inert: a duty has no life in it, it is always immobile and imbecile, because whenever anyone tries to do his so-called duty, he always finds himself in opposition to others. This contradiction ultimately derives from the demands of materiality in us. To sum up what I have been saying in a sentence: my aim in the second volume of the *Critique* was precisely a study of the paradoxical object which is an institutional ensemble that is perpetually detotalized.

There is another dimension of the Critique *which must be striking for any new reader of it today. The book in some respects appears an anticipation of two of the major historical events of recent years, the May Revolt in France and the Cultural Revolution in China. There are long analyses of the dialectical relationship between class, cadres, trade-unions and political party during factory occupations, taking 1936 as a model, which often seem to prefigure the trajectory of the French proletariat in May 1968. At the same time, there is a passage where you evoke the official parades in Tien An Minh Square in the Pekin of the early 60s as a sort of pyramidal 'mineralization of man', whereby a bureaucratic order manipulates dispersed series beneath it to confer on them a false semblance of groups. Do you then today interpret the Cultural Revolution as an attempt to reverse the deterioration of the Chinese Revolution into a set of bureaucratically institutionalized groups manipulating passive masses, by a sort of gigantic 'apocalypse' throughout China which recreates 'fused groups' such as once made the Long March and the People's War—to use the language of the* Critique?

I should say that I regard myself as very inadequately informed about the Cultural Revolution. The specific level of the phenomenon is that of ideology, culture and politics—in other words, superstructures which are the higher instances of any dialectical scale. But what happened at the level of infrastructures in China which led to the initiation of this movement in the superstructures? There must have been determinate contradictions at the base of the Chinese socialist economy which produced the movement for a return to something like a perpetual fused group. It is possible that the origins of the Cultural Revolution are to be found in the conflicts over the Great Leap Forward, and the investment policies undertaken at that time: Japanese Marxists have often maintained this. But I nevertheless must confess that I have not succeeded in understanding the causes of the phenomenon in its totality. The idea of a perpetual apocalypse is naturally very attractive—but I am convinced that it is not exactly this, and that the infrastructural reasons for the Cultural Revolution must be sought.

You do not think that the Sino-Soviet conflict was a crucial determinant? Part of the Chinese leadership appears to have consciously been determined to avoid any reproduction of the present state of the USSR in China. Is it necessary to assume insurmountable contradictions within the Chinese economy to explain the Cultural Revolution?

I certainly do not think that the Cultural Revolution is in any way a mechanical reflection of infrastructural contradictions: but I think that to understand its total meaning one should be able to reconstruct the precise moment of the historical process and of the economy at which it exploded. It is perfectly clear, for instance, that Mao was virtually marginalized for a certain time and that he has now reassumed power. This change is undoubtedly linked to internal Chinese conflicts, which go back at least to the Great Leap Forward.

Equally striking are the contradictions within the Cultural Revolution. There is a central discordance between the unleashing of mass initiatives and the cult of the leader. On the one side, there is the perpetual maintenance of the fused group with unlimited personal initiatives within it, with the possibility of writing anything in big-character posters, even 'Chou En Lai to the gallows'—which did, in fact happen in Pekin; on the other side, there is the fetishization of the little red book, read aloud in waiting rooms, in airplanes, in railway stations, read before others who repeat it in chorus, read by taxi-drivers who stop their cab to read it to passengers—a hallucinating collective catechism which resounds from one end of China to the other.

Your own analysis of the fundamental reason for the degradation of groups into a series in the Critique *is that scarcity ultimately renders inevitable the fall of any collective project into the practico-inert. China remains a very poor country, with a low level of development of productive forces. Your own account of the reign of scarcity leads to the conclusion that it is impossible to abolish bureaucracy in such a country; any attempt to overcome bureaucratic degradation of the revolution will inevitably be profoundly marked by the objective limits imposed by scarcity. This line of argument would explain the bureaucratic safety-rails, whether institutional like the army or ideological like the cult of personality, which trammel mass initiative in China?*

It is evident that completely untrammelled initiatives can lead to a sort of madness. Because the free and anarchic development of the individual—not the social individual of the future, but the free practical organism of today—may not endanger his own reason, but can endanger a society. But to insist on his total freedom within a fused group and at the same time to put pebbles in his head, called the Thoughts of Mao, is not to create a whole man. The two halves of the process are in complete contradiction.

Perhaps the paradox of a cultural revolution is that it is ultimately impossible in China, where it was invented, but is somewhat more possible in the advanced countries of the West?

I think that is correct. With one qualification: is a cultural revolution possible without making *the* revolution? French youth during May wanted a cultural revolution—what was missing for them to achieve one? The ability to make a real revolution. In other words, a revolution which is no way initially cultural, but is the seizure of power by violent class struggle. Which is not to say that the idea of cultural revolution in France was merely a mirage: on the contrary, it expressed a radical contestation of every established value of the university and society, a way of looking at them as if they had already perished. It is very important that this contestation be maintained.

What were the main lessons of the May Revolt for you?

I have always been convinced that the origins of May
lie in the Vietnamese Revolution. For the French students who unleashed the process of May, the
Vietnamese war was not merely a question of taking
the side of the National Liberation Front or the people
of Vietnam against US imperialism. The fundamental
impact of war on European or US militants was its
enlargement of the field of the possible. It had previously seemed impossible that the Vietnamese could
resist successfully such an enormous military machine
and win. Yet that is what they did and by doing so they
completely changed the horizon of French students,
among others: they now knew that there were possibilities that remained unknown. Not that everything was
possible, but that one can only know something is
impossible once one has tried it and failed. This was a
profound discovery, rich in its eventual consequences
and revolutionary in the West.

Today, over a year later, it is clear that to a certain
extent we have discovered the impossible. In particular, as long as the French Communist Party is the

largest conservative party in France, and as long as it
has the confidence of the workers, it will be impossible
to make the free revolution that was missed in May.
Which only means that it is necessary to pursue the
struggle, however protracted it may be, with the same
persistence as the Vietnamese, who after all are continuing to fight and continuing to win.

*May was not a revolution: it did not destroy the bourgeois
state. To make the revolution next time, organization will be
necessary to co-ordinate and lead the struggle. What sort of
political organization do you judge to be the appropriate
instrument today?*

It is obvious that anarchism leads nowhere, today as
yesterday. The central question is whether in the end
the only possible type of political organization is that
which we know in the shape of the present CP's: hier-
archical division between leadership and rank-and-file,
communications and instructions proceeding from
above downwards only, isolation of each cell from every
other, vertical powers of dissolution and discipline,
separation of workers and intellectuals? This pattern
developed from a form of organization which was born

in clandestinity in the time of the Tsars. What are the objective justifications of its existence in the West today? Its purpose here appears merely to ensure an authoritarian centralism which excludes any democratic practice. Of course, in a civil war situation, a militarized discipline is necessary. But does a proletarian party have to resemble the present-day Communist Parties? Is it not possible to conceive of a type of political organization where men are not barred and stifled? Such an organization would contain different currents, and would be capable of closing itself in moments of danger, to reopen thereafter.

It is always true, of course, that to fight something one must change oneself into it; in other words one must become its true opposite and not merely other than it. A revolutionary party must necessarily reproduce—up to a certain limit—the centralization and coercion of the bourgeois state which it is its mission to overthrow. However, the whole problem—the history of our century is there to prove it—is that once a party dialectically undergoes this ordeal, it may become arrested there. The result is then that it has enormous difficulty in ever escaping from the bureaucratic rut which it initially accepted to make the revolution against a bureau-cratic–military machine. From that moment on, only a cultural revolution against the new order can prevent a degradation of it. It is not a benevolent reform that is occurring in China today, it is the violent destruction of a whole system of privilege. Yet we know nothing of what the future will be in China. The danger of a bureaucratic deterioration will be powerfully present in any Western country, if we succeed in making the revolution: that is absolutely inevitable, since both external imperialist encirclement and the internal class struggle will continue to exist. The idea of an instant and total liberation is a utopia. We can already foresee some of the limits and constraints of a future revolution. But he who takes these as an excuse not to make the revolution and who fails to struggle for it now, is simply a counter-revolutionary.

Abroad, you are often seen as classical product of French university culture. The university system in which you were educated and made your early career, was the exact target of the first

explosion which set off the upheaval of May. What is your judg-
ment of it now?

It is certainly true that I am a product of this system,
and I am very aware of it: although I hope I am not
only that. When I was a student, only a very small elite
got to university, and if one had the additional 'luck' to
get into the Ecole Normale, one had every material
advantage. In a sense the French university *system*
formed me more than its professors, because in my
time the latter, with only one or two exceptions, were
very mediocre. But the system, above all the Ecole
Normale, I accepted as absolutely natural: son and
grandson of petty-bourgeois intellectuals, it never
occurred to me to question it. The lectures of the *cours*
magistral seemed idiotic to us, but only because the
teachers who gave it had nothing to tell us. Later, others saw that the lecture course itself was irredeemable.
We merely abstained from ever going to the Sorbonne:
only once, when law students threatened to invade it,
did we go to the lectures there—otherwise never. Most
of the Ecole Normale students of my time were very
proud if they became *agregés*, for instance (although

there were a few who thought the hierarchy of *agregés* and *licenciés* was monstrous). Nizan was an exception, of course. He detested the Ecole Normale, for very good reasons—its class function in creating a privileged élite. Although he was academically 'successful', he never, never fitted into the system. By the third year he was in such a state of malaise that he escaped to Aden. Of course, this was related to neurotic problems in his personal history, but the fundamental fact was that he could not breathe within these institutions designed to perpetuate a monopoly of knowledge.

What is your view of a correct Marxist practice within the institutions of bourgeois culture—the educational system— after May?

Is a positive revolutionary culture conceivable today? For me, this is the most difficult problem posed by your question. My frank opinion is that everything within bourgeois culture that will be surpassed by a revolutionary culture will nevertheless ultimately also be preserved by it. I do not believe that a revolutionary culture will forget Rimbaud, Baudelaire or Flaubert, merely because they were very bourgeois and not exactly friends of the people. They will have their place in any future socialist culture, but it will be a *new* place determined by new needs and relations. They will not be great principal values, but they will be part of a tradition reassessed by a different praxis and a different culture.

But how can they be reassessed today, when a revolutionary culture does not exist? They have only one place within existing society—the site assigned to them by bourgeois culture. What is the 'correct use' of Rimbaud for a young socialist militant in Vincennes or Nanterre? The question is unanswerable. It is true that a certain number of university intellectuals of an older generation became revolutionaries within a society that dispensed this culture to them. But the situation has changed radically since then. To take only the material conditions of a university education: in my time an orthodox lecture course was trundled out to perhaps 15 or 20 people. It was less shocking, because it could formally be contested: a student could interrupt and say he disagreed, and the lecturer would tolerate this because it hid the completely authoritarian character

of the whole course. Today, there are 100 or 200 students where there were once 15. There is no longer
any chance of this. Where it was once possible to turn
bourgeois culture against itself, showing that Liberty,
Equality and Fraternity had become their opposites,
today the only possibility is to be against bourgeois
culture. For the traditional system is collapsing. The
Baccalaureat in France is something incredible, in its
antiquation. In Rouen-Le Havre recently, the subject of
the philosophy paper was 'Epictetus said to a disciple:
"Live Hidden". Comment' Can you imagine—giving a
question like that to school-children of 16 in this day
and age! Not only the reference is outrageous, of
course. 10 percent to 20 percent of the candidates
thought *Vis Caché* (Live Hidden) was Vices Caches
(Hidden Vices), imagining perhaps that this was
ancient orthography, and interpreted the quotation to
mean: 'Hide your Vices'. They then developed at
length the idea of Epictetus along the lines 'if you have
vices, satisfy them, but secretly.' The funniest, and sad-
dest thing of all is that they approved the formula of
Epictetus! 'For it is like that in society, one can have a
vice, but one should practise it in solitude.' Innocent

answers, showing what bourgeois morality is in fact like; pitiful answers because these pupils obviously thought 'Epictetus must be famous, if I criticize him I might get 4 out of 20 and fail, the only thing to do is to agree with him.' There is no relationship, no context whatever between these young people and their teachers. Bourgeois culture in France is destroying itself. Thus for the moment, regardless of the eventual future, I believe that a radical negation of the existing culture is the only possible option for young militants—a negation which will often take the form of violent contestation.

Are you going to write a sequel to Les Mots? *What are your future plans?*

No, I don't think that a sequel to *Les Mots* would be of much interest. The reason why I produced *Les Mots* is the reason why I have studied Genet or Flaubert: how does a man become someone who writes, who wants to speak of the imaginary? This is what I sought to answer in my own case, as I sought it in that of others. What could there be to say of my existence since 1939? How I became the writer who produced the particular works I have signed. But the reason why I wrote *La Nausée* rather than some other book is of little importance. It is the birth of the decision to write that is of interest. Thereafter, what is equally interesting are the reasons why I was to write exactly the contrary to what I wanted to write. But this is another subject altogether—the relationship of a man to the history of his time. Thus what I will write one day is a political testament. The title is perhaps a bad one, since a testament implies the idea of giving advice; here it will simply be the end of a life. What I would like to show is how a man comes to politics, how he is caught by them, and how he is remade other by them; because you must remember that I was not made for politics, and yet I was remade by politics so that I eventually had to enter them. It is this which is curious. I will recount what I did politically, what mistakes I committed, and what resulted from it. In doing so, I will try to define what constitutes politics today, in our own phase of history.

INTERVIEWED BY PERRY ANDERSON, RONALD FRASER AND QUINTIN HOARE.

[Originally published in *New Left Review* I/58, November–December 1969, pp. 43–66.]

SIMONE DE BEAUVOIR QUESTIONS
JEAN-PAUL SARTRE

Well, Sartre, I want to probe your views on the woman ques -
tion. Mainly because you have never expressed yourself on the
subject, and this in fact is the first thing I want to ask you
about. How is it that you have talked about all the oppressed
groups—workers, blacks in Orphée noir, *Jews in*
Réflexions sur la question juive—*but have never men -*
tioned women? How do you explain that?

I think it comes from my childhood. As a child I was
mostly in the company of women: my grandmother
and mother gave me a lot of attention, and then I was
surrounded by little girls. So that to some extent girls
and women were my natural milieu, and I have always
thought that there was some sort of woman inside me.

Your having been surrounded by women cannot have pre - vented you from grasping their oppression as an important phenomenon.

I used to sense that my grandmother was oppressed by my grandfather, but I did not really work out what it meant. As a widow, my mother was oppressed by her parents, but as much by her mother as by her father.

But you are an adult! Why have you neglected the oppression of which women are victims?

I was not aware of it as a general phenomenon.I only saw individual cases. Lots of them, of course. But each time, I saw the imperialism as an individual fault in the man and a certain submissiveness as a character trait of the woman.

Could one not say that many men—and women as well, I was like that for a long time myself—have a sort of blind spot about women? Relations between men and women are taken so much as given that they seem natural, and in the end are not noticed. It rather reminds me of what used to happen in ancient Greek democracy, where people professing ideas of reciprocity nevertheless did not find slavery remarkable. It seems to me that in future centuries people will regard the way in which women are treated in our society today with as much astonishment as we regard slavery in the Athenian democracy, for example.

I think you are right. When I was young, I believed in male superiority, which did not rule out some form of equality between the sexes. It seemed to me that in social life women were treated as the equals of men. In some cases, men were haughty, arrogant and authoritarian in their relations with their wives: my stepfather, for example. I simply saw this as a trait of character.

But you have just said that in your many relationships with women, you saw them as both equal and unequal. Do you mean what you once said to me, that given their oppression women are the equals of men, even if they are not equal? What I mean is, as it is difficult for a woman to have as much culture, knowledge and freedom as a man, you can see a woman as an equal even if she lacks culture, freedom and other qualities?

That is part of it. I considered she had a certain type of feelings, and a way of being, that I recognized in myself. I felt much more comfortable chatting with women than with men. With men, the conversation always degenerates into shop. You always get round to talking about the economic situation or the Greek aorist, depending on whether you are a businessman or a teacher. But it is unusual, for example, to be able to sit on a café terrace and talk about the weather outside, the passers-by, the way the street looks—all things I have always done with women and which gave me an impression of equality with them. Although, of course, it was I who led the conversation. I led it, because I had decided to lead it.

But there was an element of machismo *in the fact that it was you who led the conversation, that it was normal for you to lead. Besides, I must say that on a re-reading, one can find traces of* machismo, *even of phallocracy, in your works as a whole.*

You are exaggerating a bit. But I am prepared to believe it is true.

But you did not feel yourself that you were being macho?

In a way, yes, since it was I who put relations on one footing or another—only if the woman agreed, of course. But it was I who made the first moves. And I did not perceive the *machismo* as something stemming from my condition as a male. I took it to be a personal characteristic of mine.

That is curious, since you were the first to say that psychology, interiority, is always only the internalization of a situation.

Yes. I was in the general situation of a man of our time in relation to women. I took it to be an individual superiority. I admit, too, do not forget, that I attrib-uted to myself a good deal of superiority over my age and sex group: in other words, over a lot of men.

You mean that the idea of superiority did not seem to you to be peculiar to your relations with women, because you had it with everyone?

If you like. But there was a specific element in it, because it was linked to feeling. It would be interesting to study superiority as perceived through a sentiment. What does it mean to love someone while feeling supe-rior to them, and to what extent is it a contradiction?

Well, what I find most interesting there is that although you were fond of saying that you are just anybody, you did not feel that your machismo *was just anybody's.*

But the particular *machismo* of an individual. Do not imagine that I have regarded myself as just anybody all my life. I have only done so since the age of 40; that is when I wrote it, and it is still what I think.

To get back to machismo, *we should not over-simplify. After all, you vigorously encouraged me to write* The Second Sex; *and when the book was finished you accepted all the ideas in it, while people like Camus, for example, practically flung it in my face. Furthermore, it was then that I discovered* machismo *in a number of men whom I had believed gen - uinely democratic, in matters of sex as in relation to society as a whole.*

Yes, but we ought to say first of all that in our relation-ship, I have always considered you as an equal.

I would say that you have never oppressed me, and that you have never claimed any superiority over me. *To understand the nuances of your* machismo, *it is important to see that we have never had the superior-inferior relations which are com - mon between men and women.*

It is through our relationship that I have learned—understood—that there are relationships between man and woman which demonstrate the profound equality between the sexes. I did not consider myself superior to you, or more intelligent, or more active, so I put us on the same level. We are equals. Oddly enough, I think in a way this re-inforced my *machismo*, because it allowed me to go back to being *macho* with other women. Nevertheless, the equality between us did not seem to me simply the accidental equality of two individuals, but appeared to reveal the profound equality of the two sexes.

Right. That said, you accepted The Second Sex. *It did not change you at all. Perhaps I should add that it did not change me either, for I think we had the same attitude at that time. We had the same attitude in that we both believed that the socialist revolution would necessarily bring about the emancipation of women. We have been disillusioned since then, because we have seen that women are not really equal to men in the USSR, Czechoslovakia or any of the countries called socialist that we know. This, incidentally, is what decided me, around 1970, to take up an openly feminist position. What I mean by this is, to recognize the specificity of women's struggles. What is more, you followed me on this path; but I would like to know just how far. What do you think, now, of the struggle of women for their liberation? For example, how do you think it connects with the class struggle?*

I see them as two struggles of different aspect and meaning, which do not always mix. So far, the class struggle is between men. It is essentially a question of relations between men, relations concerned with power or economics. Relations between men and women are very different. No doubt there are some very important implications from the economic point of view, but women are not a class, nor are men a class in relation to women. Relations between the sexes are something else. In other words, there are two main lines of struggle for the oppressed: the class struggle and the struggle between the sexes. Of course, the two lines often coincide. For example, there is today a tendency for the class struggle and the struggle between the sexes to coincide. I say there is a tendency, because the principles of the two struggles are not articulated in the same way. The wife of the bourgeois and the worker's wife are not opposed along precise class lines. The class division between bourgeoisie and workers only reaches women on a very secondary level. For example, one often finds relations between a bourgeois woman and her maid or housekeeper which would be unthinkable between a bourgeois factory owner or engineer and an assembly-line worker in the same factory.

What kind of relations do you mean?

Relations in which the bourgeois woman talks about her husband, her relationship with her husband, her house . . .There can be a complicity between two women belonging to different classes. I think that a bourgeois woman, except in specific cases where she is the head of a business, for example, does not belong to the bourgeois class. She is bourgeois through her husband.

You mean a traditional bourgeois woman?

Yes, one who lives with her parents, under her father's authority, until she marries a man who takes over from her father, softening his principles slightly. She has no opportunity to affirm herself as belonging to the masculine class, the bourgeois class. Of course, in many cases she assimilates bourgeois principles. Of course, the wife of a bourgeois usually seems to be a bourgeois woman. She often expresses the same opinions as her husband, more forcefully even. And to an extent she imitates her husband's behaviour in her relations with 'inferiors'. For example, she is ambiguous towards her housekeeper, she has a dual attitude towards her. On the one hand, there is a certain sex complicity, the truly feminine relation, in which the bourgeois woman confides in the housekeeper, who understands the confidences and may earn her employer's trust with appropriate comments. Then on the other hand there is the employer's authority, which is just an authority borrowed through her relationship with her husband.

In other words, you would accept the thesis of some women in the women's liberation movement that a bourgeois woman is bourgeois only by proxy.

Certainly, given that she never has the relation to economic and social life which a man has. She has it only by proxy. A bourgeois woman very seldom has any relations with capital. She is tied sexually to a man who does have these relations.

It is striking, too, that a bourgeois woman kept by her hus - band, who has no father to take her in if her husband wants a divorce, is forced to look for work; the work she finds will usually be very badly paid, and will hardly keep her above the condition of a proletarian.

I remember my mother's relations with money: first she got money from her husband, then from her father, then she received a proposal from another man, my stepfather, who kept her until he died. At the end of her life, she lived partly on what my stepfather had left her and partly on money that I gave her. She was supported by men from one end of her life to the other, and had absolutely no direct relation to capital.

In other words, you recognize the specificity of the women's struggle?

Absolutely. I do not believe that it stems from the class struggle.

Feminism, to me, represents one of the struggles situated out - side the class struggle, though tied in with it to a certain extent. There are plenty of others these days: the national struggles in Britanny and Languedoc, for example, which do not coincide with the class struggle.

They are more closely tied to it, though.

The young soldiers' revolt is another thing which is different from the class struggle. I believe there are a lot of movements today which are related to the class struggle but at the same time independent of it, or at any rate cannot be reduced to it.

They would need to be examined individually. I recognize that the specificity of women's struggle against men is not at all the struggle of the oppressed classes against their oppressors. It is something else. Though the essence of women's struggle against men is indeed a struggle against oppression, because men try to imprison women in a subordinate position.

What importance do you give to this feminist struggle which you recognize as such? Would you maintain the old distinc - tion between primary and secondary contradictions, and would you regard the women's struggle as secondary?

No, I regard women's struggle as primary. For centuries, this struggle has emerged only in individual relationships, in every home. The sum total of these individual struggles is now building a more general struggle. It has not reached everyone; I would even say that the majority of women do not realize that it is in their interests to join their individual struggles to a more general struggle, that of all women against all men. This general struggle has not yet reached its full dimensions.

There are areas in which women feel themselves to be deeply involved, without being very aware of their significance. The battle over abortion was led in the first instance by a handful of intellectuals. When we signed the Manifesto of the 343, there were still very few of us; but it aroused such a resonance, among all women, that in the end the new law on abortion was extracted from the government. Not a wholly satisfactory law, far from it, but a victory all the same.

Yes, but remember that a lot of men are also in favour of abortion. It is often the man who pays for an abortion. A married man who has a mistress, for example, has no wish for a child by her.

I think you are being a bit optimistic about men's solicitude for pregnant women. In a considerable number of cases, the man vanishes completely, giving neither money nor moral support. The battle for abortion was won by women.

Up to a point, at present, yes. But all the same, it was a male parliament that voted the law through; an instance of a certain complicity between the sexes.

That said, there are many women who are not conscious of their oppression in a positive way, who think it natural to do all the housework themselves and to have almost sole respon - sibility for the children. What do you think of the problem confronting women in the women's liberation movement when they meet, let us say, working women who on the one hand work in a factory where they are exploited, and on the other hand are exploited at home by their husbands? Do you think they should be made aware of this domestic oppression, or not?

Certainly. But it is obvious that at the present time there is a distance between bourgeois or petty-bour- geois women and working-class women. Their basic interests are the same, and moreover they may as women be able to communicate with one another, but they remain separate. This results in large part from the class difference separating their husbands, and from the fact that they are obliged to reflect the social ideas of their bourgeois or working-class husbands. This is the main distinction between bourgeois women and working-class women, because the basic way of life—managing the home, child care and so on—is found in varying degrees on both sides.

Yes. Only the working-class woman who works herself is sub - jected to both oppressions. My specific question, which I asked for practical reasons, was this: should the woman be, as it were, set against her husband, although he often seems to her to be her only refuge from oppression by her employers?

There is a contradiction there. But you have to remember that it is the opposite of what is usually said. The major contradiction is that of the struggle between the sexes, and the minor contradiction is the class struggle. Where women find themselves subject to a double oppression, the sex struggle takes first place. I think working-class women should try to devise a synthesis, which would have to vary according to the case, between the workers' struggle and the women's struggle, without underrating the importance of either. I do not think this will be easy, but it is a direction in which progress is possible.

Yes. But I remember a discussion we had after seeing Karmitz's Coup sur coup. *There were women from the women's liberation movement and working-class women in the audience. When we talked about their oppression by their husbands, they gave us to understand very clearly that they*

felt a great deal closer to a worker husband than to a bour -
geois woman.

In one sense that seems obvious. But the question is
whether the problems of bourgeois women are not the
same as those confronting working women. Because as
we have seen, a bourgeois woman abandoned by her
husband, or simply widowed, is in danger of joining
the working-class woman, or in any case the petty-
bourgeois woman, in very badly paid work.

You can see a connection between the class struggle and the
struggle between the sexes when women start movements
involving professional demands. I know two examples of this.
One of them was a strike at Troyes two or three years ago .
The women workers leading the strike told members of the
women's liberation movement, quite spontaneously and very
vehemently: 'Now that I understand what it means to revolt,
I'm not going to be trampled on at home any more. My old
man had better not try playing the gaffer.' Similarly, the
women employees of the Nouvelles Galeries *at Thionville,*
who had a very tough strike, expressed some extremely femi -
nist views, explaining that they were just becoming aware of
the double exploitation and rejected both aspects of it. In your

opinion, then, can we conclude that it is a good thing to help women to open their eyes, even at the risk of creating a cer - tain tension which could be painful for them?

Of course. It seems to me impossible to expect part of the population to give up one of the essential human struggles. Since women are victims, they must become conscious of the fact.

I agree. They must become conscious of it, they must find means to struggle and must not feel isolated in their struggle. Now there is another question I would like to ask you, one which seems to me very important and which is discussed in the women's liberation movement: what relationship should be established between advancement, if you like to call it that, and equality? On the one hand, we are in favour of an egali - tarian society and the abolition not only of the exploitation of man by man but of hierarchies, privileges and so on. On the other hand, we want to have access to the same qualifications as men, to start off with the same chances, to have equal pay, the same career opportunities, the same chance of reaching the top of the hierarchy. There is a certain contradiction in this.

The contradiction exists essentially because there is a

hierarchy. If we visualize a movement—as I would like to see—getting rid of the hierarchy, then the contra-diction would vanish; in other words, women would be treated exactly the same as men. There would be a profound equality of men and women in work, and this problem would no longer exist. But we have to look at things as they are today. Men themselves today are fairly equal in subordinate jobs, jobs which are badly paid or require little specialized knowledge. But there are also very well-paid jobs, which confer a meas-ure of power and require a body of learning. It seems to me legitimate that the majority of women should unite to achieve the absolute equality of men and women on a level where hierarchies will no longer exist; and on another level, in present-day society, that they should prove through the achievements of some women that they are the equals of men even in the élite careers.

So I consider that a certain number of women, provided they belong to the same egalitarian and feminist movement, should, because they can, go right to the top of the social ladder: to show, for example, that they are not devoid of mathematical or scientific intelligence as many men claim they are, and that they are capable of doing the same jobs as men. It seems to me that these two categories of women are both essential at this moment in time, as long as it is understood that the élitist category is delegated, in a sense, by the mass of women, to prove that in the present society based on élites and injustice women, like men, can play an élite role. This seems to me necessary, because it will disarm those men who are against women on the pretext that women are inferior to them intellectually or in some other way.

You could say that it will disarm them rather than convince them. They want to believe women inferior because they want the leading role for themselves. But is there not a danger that these women may serve as an excuse? Different tendencies emerged within the women's liberation movement over the issue of Mlle Chopinet [who passed out top from the École Polytechnique]. Some, including myself, said it was a good thing that she had proved her ability, while others argued that men were going to use her as a token and say: 'But you're getting the same opportunities, as you see, you can succeed as easily as men; so don't make out you're being maintained in a situation of inferiority.' What do you think of this danger?

I think it exists, although it is easy to answer that particular male line, as you did adequately, for example, in the *Les temps modernes* special issue on women. The danger does exist, however. That is why the 'token woman' you mention is an ambiguous creature; she may be used to justify inequality, but she only exists as a delegate, in a sense, of women who want equality. Nevertheless, I believe in our present society it is impossible to ignore the fact that there are women who do men's jobs just as well as men.

After all, you could say that there is always a risk of being made an excuse, of becoming an alibi for the thing you are fighting. It is connected with the idea of 'playing so-and-so's game'. You cannot undertake anything without playing some - one's game in one way or another. For example, we do not stop writing on the pretext that even if we write against the bourgeoisie, the bourgeoisie assimilates us as bourgeois writers. So we agree that it is a good thing for women to have the highest qualifications. But I would draw a dis -

tinction between the qualification and the job; because even if women have the qualifications, should they take jobs which imply the retention of hierarchies we do not want?

I think it is impossible at present to conceive of qualifications which do not lead to jobs. In these jobs, women can introduce changes.

Something else you can say is that there are some jobs that men should refuse too. After all, a woman ought to refuse to be an Inspector-General or a Minister in the government as it is at present; and so should a man. Basically, things which are impossible for one sex are impossible for the other. But women are in great danger of finding themselves trapped, because they will exercise the power their qualifications give them in a man's world where men hold virtually all the power. One might hope, for example, that a woman doing biological research would direct her efforts towards women's problems, menstruation, contraception and so forth. In fact, she will be working in a framework previously drawn up by men; and therefore, I think, in a very delicate position, for she should not serve exclusively male interests. This leads us to another question, also a source of controversy in the women 's liberation movement: should women reject this male universe wholesale, or should they make a place in it for themselves? Should they steal the tool, or change it? I mean science just as much as language and the arts. All the values are marked with the seal of masculinity. Is it necessary, there - fore, to reject them completely and try to reinvent something radically different, starting from scratch? Or should one assimilate these values, take them over and make use of them for feminist ends? What do you think?

This poses the problem of whether there are any specifically feminine values. I notice, for example, that women's novels often try to approach the interior life of women; and that their authors make use of masculine values to describe feminine realities. There are some values peculiar to women, connected with nature, the earth, clothing, etc.; but these are secondary values, which do not correspond to any eternal feminine reality.

There, you introduce another question, the question of 'femi - ninity'. None of us accepts the idea of a feminine nature; but is it not possible, culturally, that the oppressed status of women has developed certain defects in them, and also cer - tain positive qualities, which differ from those of men?

Certainly. But they do not mean that in the more or less distant future, if feminism triumphs, these principles and this sensibility need necessarily remain in existence.

But if we feel that we possess certain positive qualities, would it not be better to communicate them to men than to eliminate them in women?

It is possible, in fact, that a good, deep and precise self-knowledge belongs more to women and less to men.

You said at the beginning that you used to prefer the company of women to that of men; is this not because, as a result of their oppression, they avoided certain male defects? You have often remarked that they were less 'comic' than men.

Absolutely. Oppression has a lot to do with it. What I mean by 'comic ' is that in so far as a man sets himself up as an average man, he comes to terms with external conditions which make him really comic. For example, in seeing my *machismo* as a personal quality and not as society's effect on me, I was comic.

You mean men are duped more easily?

More easily duped and more comic. Male society is a comic society.

Roughly speaking, because everyone is playing roles and is completely unnatural in these roles?

That's it. Perhaps women, as oppressed people, are freer than men in some ways. Their behaviour is controlled by fewer principles. They are more irreverent.

So you say you approve of the feminist struggle?

Absolutely. And I find it altogether normal that feminists do not agree among themselves on all points, that there are frictions and divisions. It is normal for a group that has reached your stage. I think, too,that they lack a mass base and that their task now is to gain one. If this condition is fulfilled, feminist struggle, in alliance with the class struggle, could turn our society upside down.

TRANSLATED BY JOHN HOWE AND ROSAMUND MULVEY

['Simone de Beauvoir questions Jean-Paul Sartre' was originally published in *L'Arc* No. 61 (1975), and is reprinted by permission, with our thanks.]

IMPERIALIST MORALITY

It has been said that Bertrand Russell's tribunal would only be able to deliver a parody of justice. It is made up of committed individuals, hostile to American policies, their verdict, it is said, known in advance. According to an English journalist, 'It will be like in Alice in Wonderland: *There will be the sentence first, and the trial afterwards'.*

Let me outline the purpose, and the limits, of our tribunal. There is no question of judging whether American policy in Vietnam is evil—of which most of us have not the slightest doubt— but of seeing whether it falls within the compass of international law on war crimes. There would be no point in condemning, in a legal sense, the onslaught of American imperialism against the countries of the Third World which attempt to escape its domination. That struggle is in fact merely the transposition, on an international level, of the class struggle, and is determined by the structure of the groups engaged in it.

Imperialist policy is a necessary historical reality. By this fact it is beyond the reach of any legal or moral condemnation. The only thing possible is to combat it; intellectually by revealing its inner mechanism, politically by attempting to disengage oneself from it (the French government, contrary to appearances, does not really attempt this), or by armed struggle. I admit that I am, like other members of the 'tribunal', a declared enemy of imperialism and that I feel myself in solidarity with all those who fight against it. Commitment, from this point of view, must be total. Each individual sees the totality of the struggle and aligns himself on one side or on the other, from motives which may range from his objective situation to a certain idea that he holds of human life. On this level one may *hate* the class enemy. But one cannot judge him in the legal sense. It is even difficult, if not impossible, so long as one keeps to the purely realistic viewpoint of the class struggle, to see one's own allies in legal terms and rigorously to define the 'crimes' committed by their governments. This was clearly shown by the problem of the Stalinist labour camps. One either delivered moral judgements on them, which were entirely beside the point, or satisfied oneself with evaluating the 'positive' and the 'negative' in Stalin's policies. Some said, 'It's positive in the last analysis' and others said, 'It's negative'. That too led nowhere.

In fact, though the development of history is not determined by law and morality—which are, on the contrary, its products—these two superstructures do exert a 'feed back' effect on that development. It is this which allows one to judge a society in terms of the criteria which it has itself established. It is therefore entirely normal to inquire, at any given moment, if such and such an action can really be judged purely in terms of utility and likely outcome, or whether it does not in fact transcend such criteria and come within the scope of an international jurisprudence which has slowly been built up.

Marx, in one of the prefaces to 'Capital', makes a remark to the effect that—We are the last people who can be accused of condemning the bourgeois, since we consider that, conditioned by the process of capital and by the class struggle, their conduct is necessary. But there are moments, all the same, when they exceed the limits.

The whole problem is to know if, today, the imperialists are exceeding the limits.

When Talleyrand says: 'It is worse than a crime, it is a mistake', he sums up very well the way in which political actions have always been considered throughout history. They might be skilful or clumsy, effective or ill-starred; they always escaped legal sanction. There was no such thing as a 'criminal policy'.

And then, at Nurenburg, in 1945, there appeared for the first time the notion of a 'political crime'. It was suspect, certainly, since it consisted in imposing the law of the conqueror upon the conquered. But the condemnation of the leaders of Nazi Germany by the Nurenburg Tribunal only had any meaning at all if it implied that any government which, in the future, committed acts which could be condemned under one or other of the articles of the Nurenburg laws, would be subject to trial by a similar tribunal. Our tribunal today merely proposes to apply to capitalist imperialism its own laws. The arsenal of jurisprudence, moreover, is not limited to the laws of Nurenburg; there was already the Briand-Kellog pact; and there are the Geneva Convention and other international agreements.

The question in this case is not one of condemning a policy in the name of history, of judging whether it is or is not contrary to the interests of humanity; it is rather a question of saying if it infringes existing laws. For example, you may criticize the present policies of France, you may be totally opposed to them, as I am, but you cannot call them 'criminal'. That would be meaningless. But you could do so during the Algerian war. Torture, the organization of concentration camps, reprisals on the civilian population, executions without trial could all be equated with some of the crimes condemned at Nurenburg. If anybody at the time had set up a tribunal like the one conceived by Bertrand Russell, I would certainly have agreed to take part in

it. Because it was not done at that time with reference
to France is no reason not to do it today with reference
to the United States.

*You will be asked by what legal right, since it is the law which
you are invoking, you are setting yourselves up as judges,
which you are not . . .*

Quite true. After that, people will say, anybody can
judge anything! And then, doesn't the project risk
falling on the one side into petit-bourgeois idealism (a
number of well-known personalities make a protest in
the name of exalted human values) and on the other
into fascism, with a vengeance-seeking aspect to it
which recalls Arsene Lupin and the whole of fascist literature?

To this I would reply first of all that there is no question of condemning anybody to any *penalty* whatever.
Any judgment which cannot be executed is evidently
derisory. I can hardly see myself condemning President
Johnson to death. I would cover myself with ridicule.

Our aim is a different one. It is to study all the existing
documentation on the war in Vietnam, to bring for-

ward all the possible witnesses—American and Vietnamese—and to determine whether certain actions fall within the competence of the laws of which I have spoken. We will not invent any new legislation. We will merely say, if we establish it—and I cannot prejudge this—'Such and such acts, committed in such and such places, represent a violation of such and such international laws, and are, consequently, crimes. And there stand those who are responsible for them.' This would, if a real international tribunal existed, make the latter subject—by virtue, for example, of the laws applied at Nurenburg—to various sanctions. So it is not at all a question of demonstrating the indignant disapproval of a group of honest citizens, but of giving a juridical dimension to acts of international politics, in order to combat the tendency of the majority of people only to judge the conduct of a social group or of a government in expedient or in moral terms.

Does this not lead you to the view that there is a way of waging war which is to be condemned, and another which is not?

Certainly not! The onslaught of imperialism against certain peoples of the Third World is a fact which is clear to me. I oppose it with all my strength, to the limit of the feeble means at my disposal, but there is no point in my saying whether there is a good and a bad way in which it can be carried out. In fact, although the good, peaceful people in our consumer societies would like to ignore it, everywhere there is fighting, struggle; the world is in flames and we could have a world war from one moment to the next. I have to take sides in the struggle, not to humanize it. We only have to try and find out whether, in the course of this struggle, there are people who are exceeding the limits; whether imperialist policies infringe laws formulated by imperialism itself.

You might of course ask whether it is possible to fight an imperialist war of repression without violating international laws. But that is not our business. As an ordinary citizen, as a philosopher, as a Marxist, I have the right to believe that that type of war always leads to the use of torture, to the creation of concentration camps, and so on. As a member of the Bertrand Russell Tribunal, that does not interest me. I only have to try to discover whether laws have been violated, in order to reintroduce the legal notion of international crime.

We must ask ourselves whether the views, correct ones, which we hold about politics—(that politics must be considered realistically, that they are determined by a relation of forces, that the end pursued must be taken into account)—must necessarily lead us, as they did many people during the Stalin period, to consider politics solely from the angle of expediency, and to indulge in passive complicity by only judging a government's action from a practical perspective. Does a political fact not also possess an ethico-juridical structure?

On this ground, our judgements cannot be given in advance, even if we are committed, as individuals, in the struggle against imperialism. Again, I oppose the de Gaulle government with my vote but it would never enter my head to say that Gaullist policies were criminal. One might talk indignantly of 'the crime' of the Ben Barka affair, but I do not see what law we would apply if we wanted to condemn the French government for its role in it. It is entirely different when it is a question of judging a certain act of war by the

Americans in Vietnam, a certain bombardment, a certain military operation ordered at top level. To want to set up a real tribunal and to pronounce sentences would be to act as idealists. But we have the right to meet, as citizens, in order to give renewed strength to the notion of a war crime, by showing that any policy can and must be objectively judged in terms of the legal criteria which exist.

When somebody shouts out in a meeting: 'The war in Vietnam is a crime' we are in the realm of emotion. This war is certainly contrary to the interests of the vast majority of people, but is it *legally* criminal? This is what we will try to determine. We cannot say in advance what our conclusions will be.

Some people will reproach you for not judging the Vietnamese at the same time as the Americans, and will say that war crimes are committed by both sides.

I refuse to place in the same category the actions of an organization of poor peasants, hunted, obliged to maintain an iron discipline in their ranks, and those of an immense army backed up by a highly industrialized country of 200 million inhabitants. And then, it is not

the Vietnamese who have invaded America nor who
have rained down a deluge of fire upon a foreign
people. In the Algerian war, I always refused to place
on an equal footing the terrorism by means of bombs
which was the only weapon available to the Algerians,
and the actions and exactions of a rich army of half a
million men occupying the entire country. The same is
true in Vietnam.

*Can this possibility which will be offered you during the
'trial', of bringing to light legal norms which can be applied
to the policies of any government, debouch on to wider opposition to American policies in Vietnam?*

Of course. But that will only be able to come afterwards. It is on the basis of the results of our inquiry—if
it terminates in a condemnation—that it will be possible to organize demonstrations, meetings, marches,
signature campaigns. Our first task will be one of education, of information and our hearings will naturally
be public.

We have been reproached with petit bourgeois legalism. It is true, and I accept that objection. But who are
we trying to convince? The classes who are engaged in

the struggle against capitalism and who are already convinced (crimes or no crimes) that it is necessary to fight to the bitter end against imperialism? Or that very broad fringe of the middle class which, at the moment, is undecided? It is the petit bourgeois masses which must today be aroused and shaken, since their alliance with the working class—even from a purely local political point of view—is to be desired. And it is by means of legalism that their eyes can be opened. Besides it is no bad thing either to remind the working class, who too often have been led to think only in terms of immediate effects, that every historical action has an ethico-juridical structure. In the post-Stalin period in which we live, it is very important to try to highlight that structure.

How do you explain the fact that the demonstrations against the war in Vietnam have been more numerous and more vigorous in West Germany, in England, in Italy and in Belgium than in France?

In France, it is true, there does exist a certain impermeability in the consciousness of the petit-bourgeoisie, and even to some extent in that of the working-class.

This comes, I believe, from the fact that we are only just emerging from a long period of colonial wars. For a very long time we were 'blocked' on all problems of world importance—particularly those of the Third World—because we were the oppressors in Indo-China, and then in Algeria. It was an epoch, you will recall, in which the whole world was becoming anxious about the development of nuclear weapons. The French, for their part, never gave it a thought. They never understood that their country, which harboured American bases on its territory, would be annihilated just like other countries in case of nuclear war. They never understood it because their attention was continuously engaged by colonial problems.

There is another reason for French apathy—the confusion which de Gaulle succeeds in creating when he passes off as a genuine anti-imperialist policy what is, in fact, a purely verbal affirmation of independence. The Phnom-Penh speech was only fine words since de Gaulle, while condemning American policies, does not give himself within France the economic means of escaping American tutelage.

But the fact that de Gaulle is the only head of a capitalist state who denounces the policies of the United
States gives the French a good conscience. The same
citizen who, hostile to Algerian independence, was still
only too happy that a venerated leader should put an
end to a war impossible to win, is today very pleased
that the definitive words of the great man, with whom
he identifies, should supply a justification for his pas-
sivity: 'Since de Gaulle is taking such a firm stand on
Vietnam, it is useless for me to do more'.

If the parties of the left were united, they would have
to discover through experience that the Gaullist ambi-
tion to make France into a serious adversary of
American imperialism has no meaning, since it is not
based on an internal policy capable of genuinely free-
ing us from the grasp of the Americans.

Today France is nothing but a rebellious slave, still subject to American authority. The headquarters of Nato
will have to set itself up somewhere else, maybe, but
the Americans can put French workers out of work
where and when they wish; they can paralyse our economy merely by withdrawing their computers; they can

exert enormous pressure against which we are defenceless.

The first point of a left programme would have to be the need to combat, by means of a policy of priority investments—a great proportion of them public ones—the invasion of American capital. It would be very difficult, I know, and France could not do it alone. She would have to make use of the Common Market and to be able to induce her partners to adopt the same policy. They too, for the moment, are dominated by American economic power; but certain countries— Italy, for instance—could be brought to revise their attitude if France practised a policy of genuine economic independence.

For the moment, we are still waiting for the left to unite. And I do not see any bridging over of the gulf between the upholders and the opponents of the Atlantic Pact. The problem is partly concealed because the communists have made some concessions for the elections; but it remains posed and continues to paralyse the left. We had a perfect example of this when Guy Mollet, last spring, wanted to put down a motion of censure directed against the government's foreign policy. The communists were embarrassed because certain aspects of that policy suit them, and they said, 'Let us condemn instead the government's policies as a whole, showing that it is no more satisfactory at home than abroad.' Guy Mollet refused.

In my opinion, opposition to the Atlantic Pact ought to be the main criterion of a left policy. I would even say that the only point in common between the abstract position of de Gaulle and what ought to be the attitude of the left, is the demand for national sovereignty. Sovereignty must be won back, not in order to defend it jealously—it would be possible to associate with other similarly sovereign countries and to set up international organizations to which certain powers could be surrendered—but in order to oppose it to American imperialism which is everywhere breaking down national structures.

Let us suppose that the left was united: what could it do in effective terms about Vietnam?

It could in the first place mobilize public opinion. It is not easy, but there are some countries where it has been achieved. In France, a strike of any size, unleashed in connection with economic objectives, but whose real motive was opposition to American policy in Vietnam, is inconceivable. In Japan—where I was recently—there was, on the October 21st, a general strike 'against American imperialism'. I don't say that it was a total success, but it took place.

The French too, of course, are 'against' the Vietnam war, but they don't feel it concerns them. They don't realize that they are in danger of being dragged into a world conflict by the development of a struggle which serves the interests of the Americans alone. De Gaulle, for his part, does realize this. I was very struck by the reaction of the Japanese to his Phnom-Penh speech. They said: 'De Gaulle was afraid.' They meant that he had suddenly come to appreciate the danger of seeing his country destroyed for something which does not concern her. It was, in fact, a speech dictated by fear, and from that point of view a good speech. But a simple cry of alarm is of no great use.

We must visualize our struggle, today, in the context of a durable American hegemony. The world is not dominated by two great powers, but by one. Peaceful coexistence, despite its very positive aspects, serves the interests of the United States. It is thanks to peaceful coexistence and to the Sino-Soviet conflict—the latter resulting to a great extent from the former—that the Americans are able to bomb Vietnam undisturbed. The socialist camp has, unquestionably, suffered a reverse as a result of the rivalries and of the policies set in motion by Khrushchev. So much so that the Americans today feel that they have a free hand, to the point where President Johnson hinted in a recent speech that he would not permit the Chinese to develop their nuclear strength beyond a certain point. This horrifying and cynical threat could not have been made if Johnson had been certain that the USSR would come to China's assistance.

This present hegemony of the United States does not, however, exclude a certain vulnerability. In default of a direct confrontation with the socialist camp—too seriously divided—the solution could come from the weariness of the mass of Americans and from the disquiet of Washington's leaders at the growing disapproval of the entire world, and in particular of all their allies.

Do you think that actions like that of David Mitchell, the young American who refused to serve in Vietnam, invoking the Nurenburg laws, could contribute to a prise de conscience on the part of the Americans?

It is precisely from the action of David Mitchell and of others that the idea of our tribunal sprang. Our inquiry, if it concludes that the United States is guilty, should allow all the young who are combating Johnson's policy to invoke, not only the laws of Nurenburg but also the judgement of a number of free men who do not represent any power, or any party. It is much better that we do not represent anything. For the neo-Nazis, the Nurenburg decisions were invalid because they were delivered by victors whose law was founded on their power. We, on the contrary, hold no mandate from any power whatsoever, and nobody will be able to say that we impose our law on people whom we hold beneath our boot. We are independent because we are weak. And our position is strong because we do not seek to send a few individuals to prison, but to reawaken in public opinion, at an ominous moment of our history, the idea that there can be policies which are objectively and legally criminal.

INTERVIEWED BY PERRY ANDERSON, RONALD FRASER AND QUINTIN HOARE.

[Originally published in *New Left Review* I/41, January–February 1967, pp. 3–10.]